Inside Eye™ INCREDIBLE CREATURES

BOOK HOUSE

This edition first published in MMXV by
Book House

Distributed by Black Rabbit Books
P.O. Box 3263
Mankato
Minnesota MN 56002

Cataloging-in-Publication Data is available
from the Library of Congress

ISBN: 978-1-906370-80-0

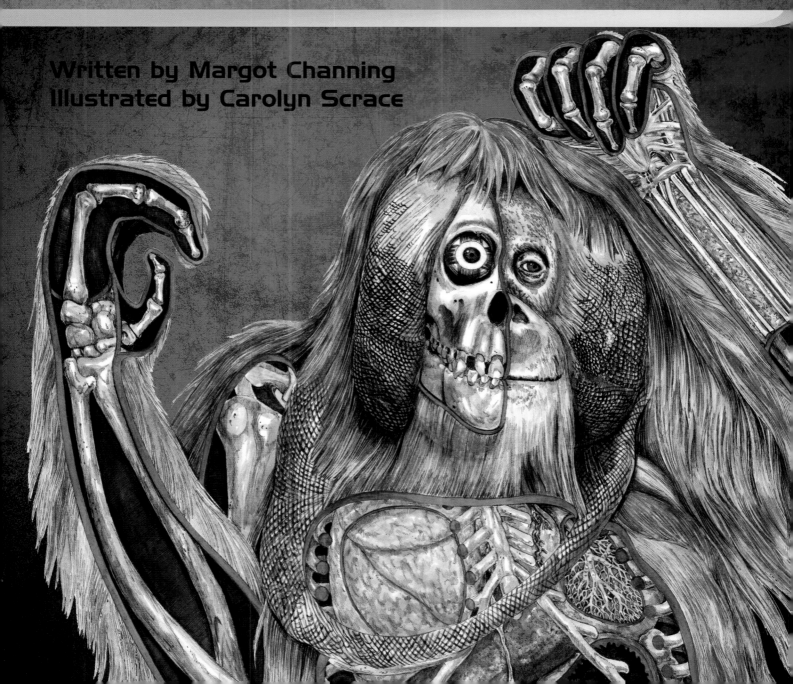

Inside Eye™ INCREDIBLE CREATURES

Written by Margot Channing

Illustrated by Carolyn Scrace

CONTENTS

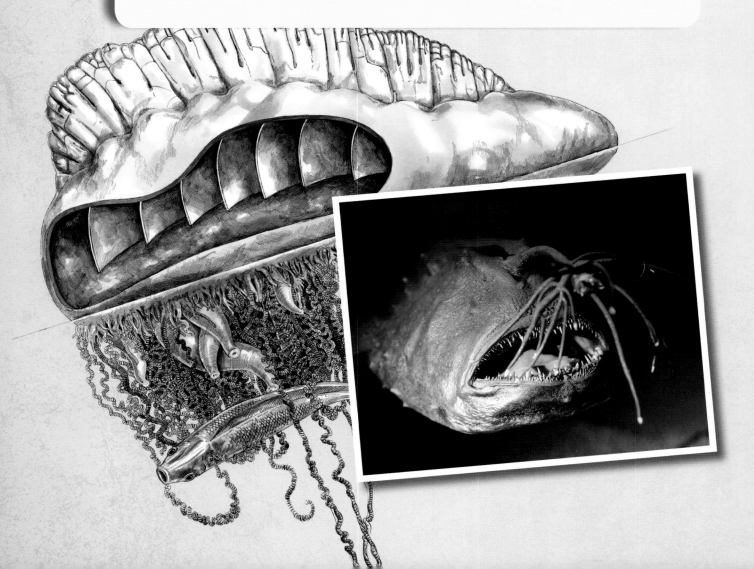

Amazing Creatures

The world is full of incredible creatures. They live on land, in oceans, rivers, and lakes, deep under our feet or up high in the sky. Some are too small to be seen, while others make us feel tiny in comparison. Some are masters of disguise or expert tunnelers, skillful builders, and lethal hunters. Every one of these creatures is amazing.

With its two huge front tusks and enormous body, the walrus is just one of Earth's many extraordinary creatures.

6

Going, Going, Gone

Some incredible creatures are facing extinction, and this is often the fault of human beings. We may be on borrowed time to see these fascinating animals. Many creatures, like the Triceratops shown here, are already extinct, but thanks to the discovery of fossilized remains, we can picture what they looked like and how they lived. There are the creatures of our imaginations—monsters and other fantastic animals that may sometimes even be based in reality.

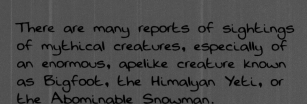

There are many reports of sightings of mythical creatures, especially of an enormous, apelike creature known as Bigfoot, the Himalyan Yeti, or the Abominable Snowman.

Inside Eye

In this book, we will look at incredible creatures of all kinds, from apes and jellyfish to single-celled protozoans, to discover where they live, how they live, what they eat, and much more. And with an amazing "inside eye" and stunning cutaway illustrations, we will show you exactly what each creature looks like—from the inside out.

Although these animals live on Earth, some, such as this frog-eating bat, look as though they are from another planet!

7

Age of the Dinosaurs

Dinosaurs, meaning "terrible reptiles," dominated Earth for more than 145 million years. Before they became extinct 65 million years ago, they roamed the deserts, plains, swamps, and forests of ferns, cycads, horsetails, and conifers. Dinosaurs were reptiles. Like modern lizards and crocodiles, they laid eggs, and had scaly skin.

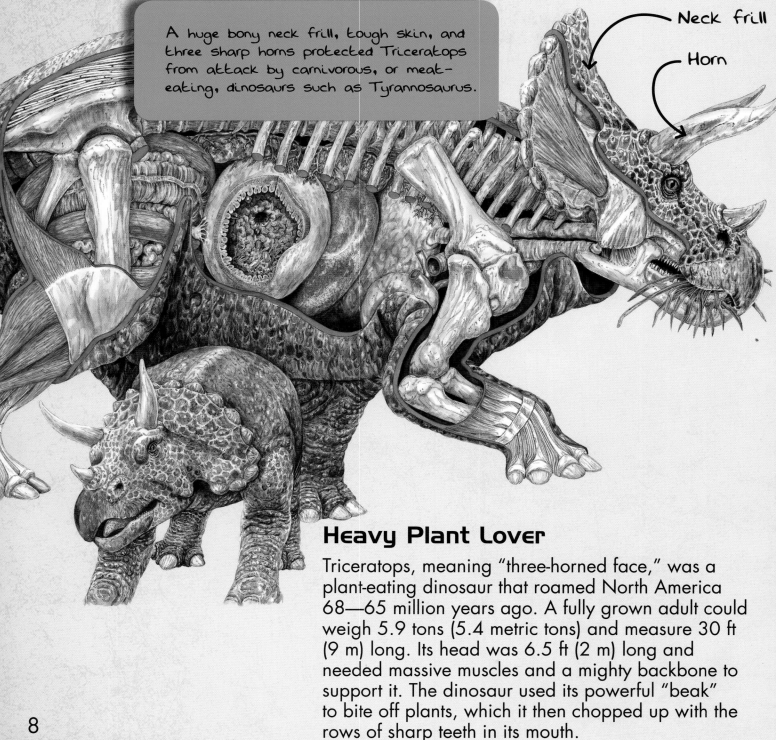

A huge bony neck frill, tough skin, and three sharp horns protected Triceratops from attack by carnivorous, or meat-eating, dinosaurs such as Tyrannosaurus.

Neck frill

Horn

Heavy Plant Lover

Triceratops, meaning "three-horned face," was a plant-eating dinosaur that roamed North America 68—65 million years ago. A fully grown adult could weigh 5.9 tons (5.4 metric tons) and measure 30 ft (9 m) long. Its head was 6.5 ft (2 m) long and needed massive muscles and a mighty backbone to support it. The dinosaur used its powerful "beak" to bite off plants, which it then chopped up with the rows of sharp teeth in its mouth.

8

Tyrannosaurus, or "tyrant reptile," was the world's largest land-living meat eater. It may have been a scavenger, attracted by the smell of decaying bodies.

Agile Limbs

At first glance, some dinosaurs look like huge versions of modern lizards. They were, in fact, quite different. Lizards have short legs that extend from each side of their bodies. This means that their movements are quite awkward. Dinosaurs, on the other hand, had long legs tucked underneath their bodies, enabling them to move efficiently and to keep their body clear of the ground.

Not all dinosaurs were huge. This is a skull of Velociraptor, or "speedy predator." This dinosaur was only 6 ft (1.8 m) long but had a sickle-like claw on its hind foot that could rip open its prey.

Early Flight

None of the dinosaurs could fly, but flying reptiles such as Pteranodon, meaning "winged and toothless," shared the planet at the same time. Pteranodon lived 85—65 million years ago and had broad wings up to 23 ft (7 m) across, which allowed it to glide for long distances.

9

Single-cell Wonders

Protozoans are tiny, single-celled creatures that slither in mud, inhabit the stomachs of cows, gyrate in drops of pond water, and ride the ocean waves. Most can be seen clearly only under a microscope. A protozoan's single cell does everything necessary to keep it alive, such as breathing, feeding, and reproducing. In contrast, our bodies are masses of billions of cells all doing different jobs.

The funnel-shaped protozoan *Stentor polymorphus* lives attached to leaves and weeds in ponds. It does not hunt for food but waits for it to drift by in the water. It moves itself by beating against the water with tiny hairs called cilia.

Nucleus

Organelle

Cilia

Watery Existence

All cells, whether human or protozoan, are made of cytoplasm, a jellylike substance surrounded by a membrane, or thin wall. Protozoans must live in wet or damp places otherwise their soft bodies shrivel up. Within each protozoan's single cell are organelles, or mini organs. The most important is the nucleus, which controls the cell and its reproduction.

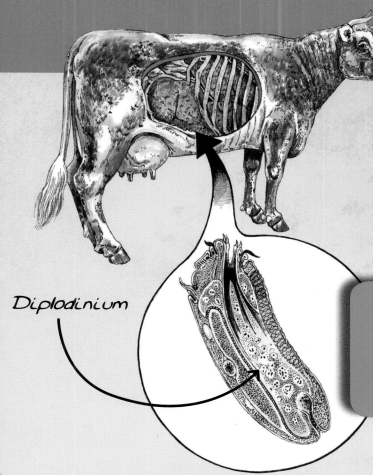

Diplodinium

Inside Job

Many single-celled creatures use the insides of other animals as a "pond." They swim in the blood and live in other tissues of the larger host animal's body. Some are parasites that feed on their host, while others help their host.

The protozoan *Diplodinium* lives in the stomach of a cow. When the cow eats grass and hay, *Diplodinium* helps break down the fibrous food, making it easier for the cow to digest.

These are single-celled organisms viewed under a microscope. These organisms survive inside the bodies of living animals.

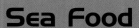

Sea Food

A delicate bell made of silica, the same substance as sand, supports the body of a radiolarian, *Dictyocysta cassis*. Radiolarians are protozoans. Together with minute plants and microscopic animals, they form part of the plankton that feeds many sea animals.

11

Spineless Seafarers

All living animals can be divided into two groups: vertebrates, those with a backbone, and invertebrates, those without a backbone. About 95 percent of animals are invertebrates. Those creatures without a backbone support their body in quite different ways. Some, such as jellyfish, are like a gas-filled bag of Jell-O. Crabs, snails, and clams have a strong outer skeleton called an exoskeleton.

The Portuguese man-of-war jellyfish has tentacles that trail more than 33 ft (10 m) below its body. Armed with powerful stinging cells, containing poisonous nematocysts, they deliver a sting that can kill.

Mouthpart

Tentacle

Sting in the Tail

Jellyfish have special stinging cells, called nematoblasts. These cells contain tiny, high-powered and deadly harpoons, called nematocysts. When a nematoblast is fired, a barbed thread twists and drills its way into an object or animal, releasing a poison. Jellyfish use nematocysts for anchorage and defense, as well as to catch food.

Clams have two hinged shells made of a chalky material. If frightened, the clams close the shells to protect their soft body.

Partly closed shell

Seabed Filters

Many adult invertebrates stay in one place for most of their lives. Instead of searching for food, they wait for food to come to them. Some invertebrates, such as giant clams, filter food from the water. They have siphons that suck in water and pump it through gills covered in mucus. These gills filter off particles that are then carried to the mouth by the beating movement of cilia.

The graceful sea butterfly is, in fact, a snail. Two long fins, called parapodia, extend from its body and act as "wings," allowing the sea butterfly to "fly" through the ocean.

Not Really a Crab

Horseshoe crabs are not related to crabs at all. They are members of a group of invertebrates called arthropods, which includes spiders and scorpions. Like its fellow group members, the horseshoe crab has a single pair of pincerlike jaws, called chelicerae.

13

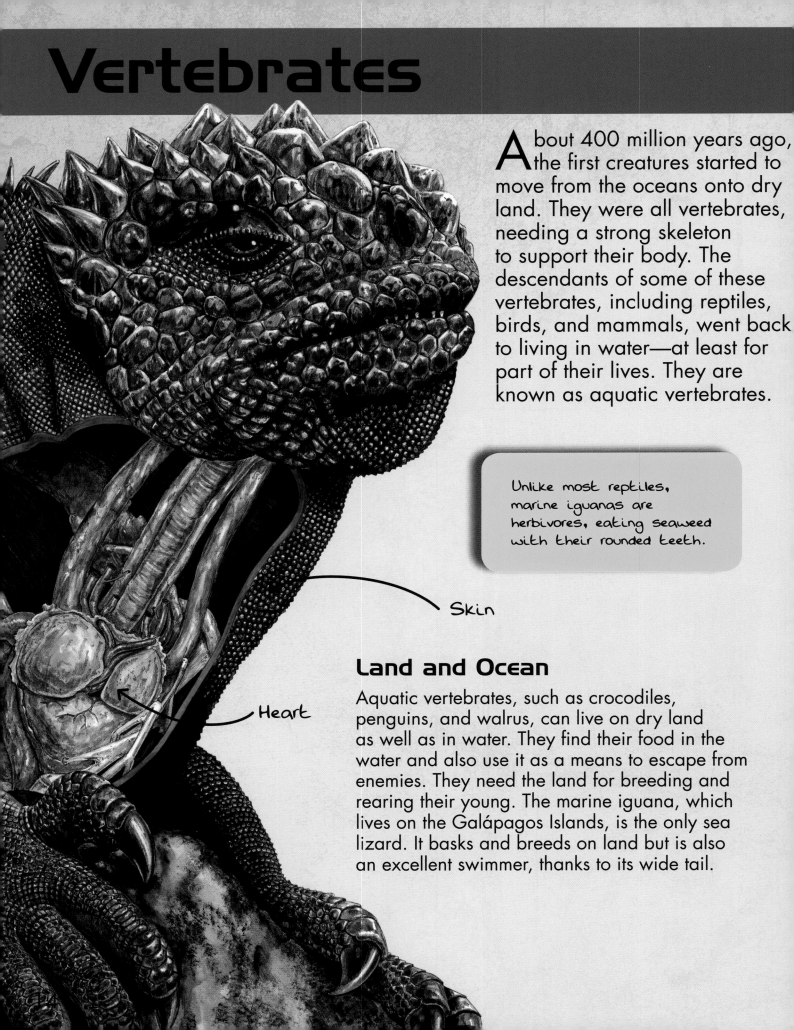

Vertebrates

About 400 million years ago, the first creatures started to move from the oceans onto dry land. They were all vertebrates, needing a strong skeleton to support their body. The descendants of some of these vertebrates, including reptiles, birds, and mammals, went back to living in water—at least for part of their lives. They are known as aquatic vertebrates.

Unlike most reptiles, marine iguanas are herbivores, eating seaweed with their rounded teeth.

Skin

Heart

Land and Ocean

Aquatic vertebrates, such as crocodiles, penguins, and walrus, can live on dry land as well as in water. They find their food in the water and also use it as a means to escape from enemies. They need the land for breeding and rearing their young. The marine iguana, which lives on the Galápagos Islands, is the only sea lizard. It basks and breeds on land but is also an excellent swimmer, thanks to its wide tail.

Walrus use their enormous tusks, which can be 3 ft (1 M) long, for fighting, as well as to haul their bulky body out of the water.

Giant Water Baby

Walrus are huge, water-loving mammals that can weigh up to 3,750 lb (1,700 kg) . They live in colonies along the Arctic coasts of North America. They spend more time in the water than they do on land. They feed, breed, and even sleep in the water. Their thick, fatty skin keeps them warm in the icy conditions.

Flipper

Turtles are reptiles that spend most of their lives in the ocean. Their large lungs allow them to submerge for more than half an hour, using their broad, paddle-like feet to swim. A turtle's body has a bony carapace, or shell, to protect its head, tail, and legs.

Shell

Underwater Flier

Penguins are flightless birds. On land they appear clumsy, waddling around on stumpy legs. Underwater, however, they "fly." Their powerful webbed feet and stubby wings propel them forward through the water at great speed.

Insect Builders

All over the world there are towering cities with roads, rooms, gardens, nurseries, stores, and air-conditioning plants—built by insects. Many species of insects live together in a colony, sharing tasks and building a communal home to protect themselves from enemies and the weather. Within each species, some insects are responsible for doing particular chores, such as gathering food and water or defending the colony.

Mound

A termite mound is one of the most complex insect structures. Miles of passages lead to food stores, nurseries, and the queen's egg-laying chamber.

Nursery

Creating Colonies

Bees, ants, wasps, and termites all live in colonies. Some wasp colonies contain only five or six individuals, while bees may have colonies of more than 60,000. Termites form the largest colonies, building nests weighing 11 tons (10 metric tons) and containing millions of individual insects.

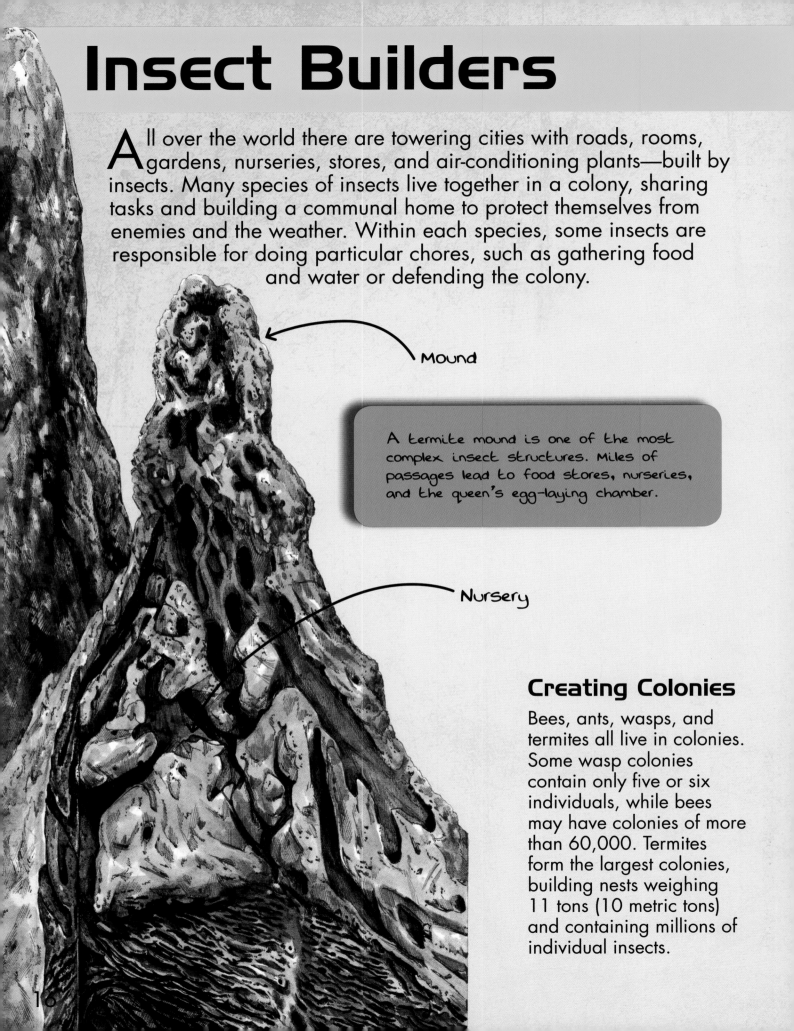

16

The single entrance to a wasp's nest makes it easier to defend. Some wasps stand guard to check who comes and goes.

Paperwork

A colony of wasps lives in a nest made out of wood. Wasps use their jaws to cut away small pieces of dead wood, which they chew and mix with saliva. The resulting mush is the basis of the delicate sheets of "paper" that gradually form the nest. Because the dead wood comes from various sources, the wasps' nest is striped with different colors.

Dead wood

Cell

Bees build combs inside their nests or in hives provided by beekeepers. A comb is formed of hundreds of hexagonal cells, built with wax secreted by glands under a bee's abdomen. They mold the wax with their jaws to form the comb, which holds honey, pollen, eggs, and young bees.

Child Labor

Tailor ants use their newly hatched offspring, or larvae, to "sew" together clusters of leaves to form nests. They use the larvae like tubes of glue, making them secrete silk to bind the leaves together.

17

Masters of Disguise

Some clever creatures use camouflage to become "invisible." They blend into their surroundings or pretend to be something they are not in order to find food, to avoid being eaten, or to find a mate. Camouflage ranges from simple color matching with a creature's habitat, to the growth of frills, scales, knobs, or lumps to imitate objects such as leaves or branches.

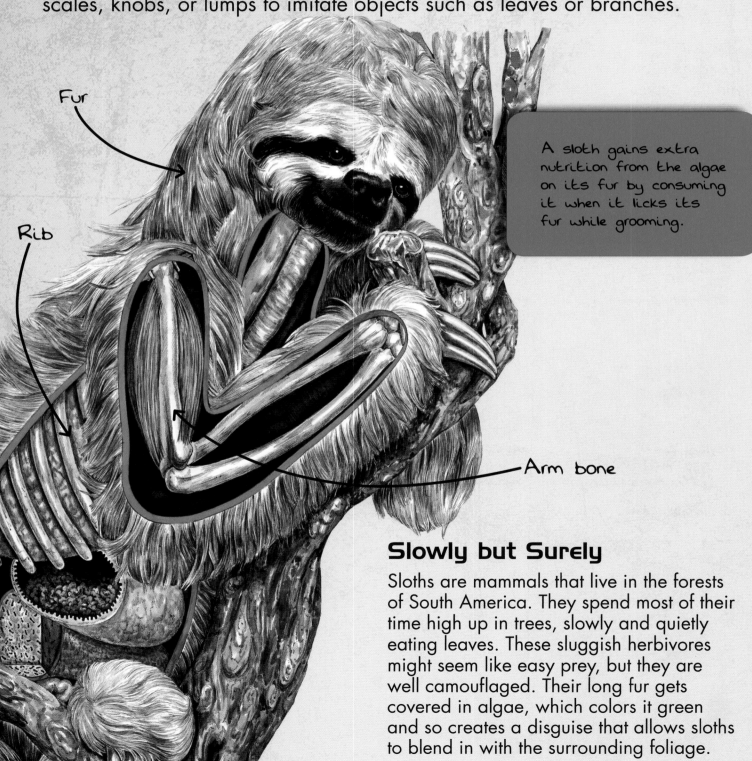

Fur

Rib

A sloth gains extra nutrition from the algae on its fur by consuming it when it licks its fur while grooming.

Arm bone

Slowly but Surely

Sloths are mammals that live in the forests of South America. They spend most of their time high up in trees, slowly and quietly eating leaves. These sluggish herbivores might seem like easy prey, but they are well camouflaged. Their long fur gets covered in algae, which colors it green and so creates a disguise that allows sloths to blend in with the surrounding foliage.

As chameleons search for insects, they move extremely slowly to avoid being seen. They catch insects with their long, sticky tongues.

Hollow Bones

Lizards creeping and climbing in tropical trees use their green, brown, and yellow skin colors to blend in with the leaves and branches. The Yemenese chameleon, which lives in the scrubby trees of the arid hills of Yemen, can change its color to hide from both its predators and prey. Special cells on its skin contain different-colored pigments. By altering the shapes of the cells, the chameleon changes color to match its background.

"Fishing rod" spine

The ugly anglerfish lies in wait for its prey on the seabed, where it looks exactly like a stone or rock. The female uses a spine protruding above its mouth like a fishing rod to lure its prey.

Life-saving Decoration

To avoid predatory fish, decorator crabs camouflage themselves. They pluck pieces of seaweed, sponge, and sea fir, chew them slowly and then attach them to their shell.

Flying Machines

To fly, a creature needs a special body with strong muscles to hold and work the wings, good eyesight, and a brain big enough to deal with the problems of flying. To lighten the load, birds also have thin skulls, beaks instead of teeth, and hollow bones. Birds' forelimbs have evolved into wings, which consist of feathers attached to the bones of the arms.

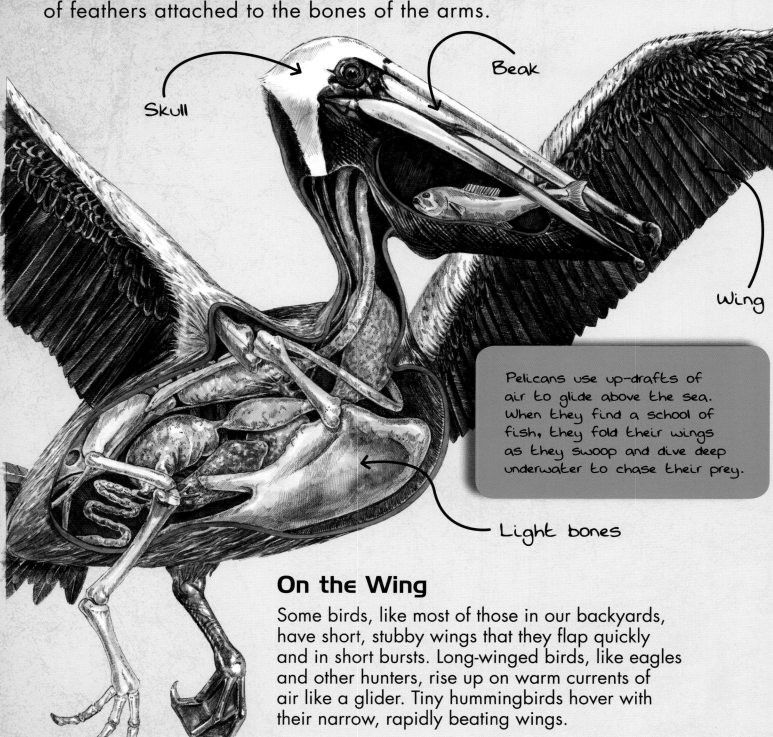

Skull

Beak

Wing

Pelicans use up-drafts of air to glide above the sea. When they find a school of fish, they fold their wings as they swoop and dive deep underwater to chase their prey.

Light bones

On the Wing

Some birds, like most of those in our backyards, have short, stubby wings that they flap quickly and in short bursts. Long-winged birds, like eagles and other hunters, rise up on warm currents of air like a glider. Tiny hummingbirds hover with their narrow, rapidly beating wings.

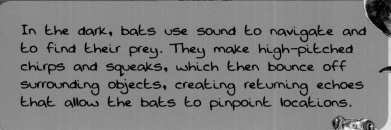

In the dark, bats use sound to navigate and to find their prey. They make high-pitched chirps and squeaks, which then bounce off surrounding objects, creating returning echoes that allow the bats to pinpoint locations.

Creature of the Night

Bats are the only mammals that can really fly. Unlike a bird's wing, the wing of a bat is made of skin stretched between the body and the bones of the fingers, hand, and arm. The bat's hooked thumbs help it grip and clamber around on trees and cave walls, where the creature rests upside down during the day. It becomes active again at dawn, dusk, and during the night.

Fits the Bill

The strange bill of the shoebill bird is ideal for catching frogs, fish, and snakes and for carrying water to its chicks. Large wings allow the bird to lift and fly with these heavy loads.

Beak

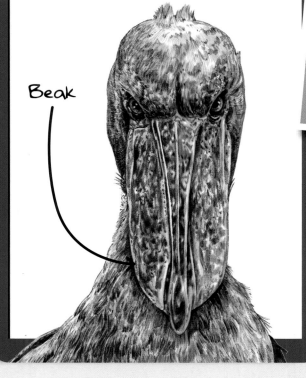

The wings of a hummingbird can beat 200 times a second. This allows the bird to hover on the spot or to move backward.

21

Endangered Animals

Stone-age people caused the extinction of mammoths and many other species through overhunting. Today, human beings are still the main threat to many creatures. Hunters kill wild animals for food, clothing, and sport and capture them for sale as pets. Colonizers can easily upset the balance of nature when they introduce rats, rabbits, and other animals to far-away places.

Flap

Strong, large hand

Male orangutans develop a fleshy pouch below the chin and flaps on either side of the face. The arms grow much longer than the legs and can span well over 6.5 ft (2 m).

Lung

Intestines

Gentle Tree Dweller

The orangutan, meaning "the old man of the trees," is an ape found only in the low-lying forests of Sumatra, Sarawak, and Borneo. Its numbers have declined sharply over the past 60 years through the loss of forests and the illegal trade in young animals. Orangutans are smuggled into Singapore and Bangkok and sold for high prices.

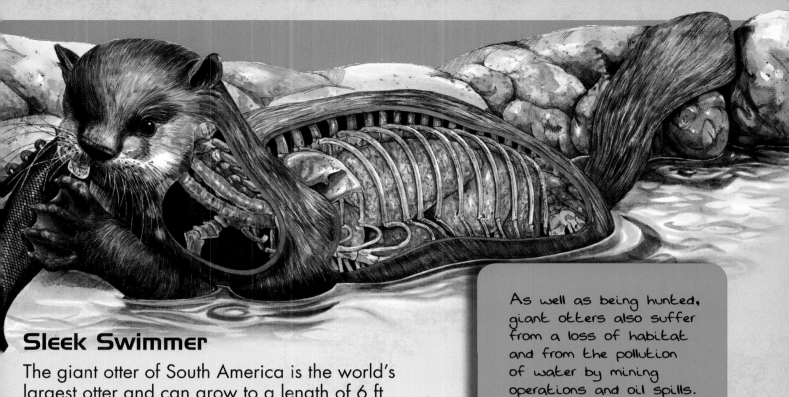

Sleek Swimmer

The giant otter of South America is the world's largest otter and can grow to a length of 6 ft (1.8 m). It thrives in slow-moving streams and rivers, where its long, sinewy body, webbed feet, and rudderlike tail make it a strong swimmer. The otter has no known predators—except for humans. Its velvety, reddish-brown fur is highly prized by illegal poachers.

As well as being hunted, giant otters also suffer from a loss of habitat and from the pollution of water by mining operations and oil spills.

The Javan rhinoceros has been hunted almost to extinction to satisfy the demand for its horn in China. Rhino horn, which is made from the same material as hair, is mistakenly thought to have magical powers.

Pet Victim

The scarlet-chested parakeet is one of the most beautiful of Australia's many parakeets. However, a huge demand for this bird as a caged pet has resulted in the deaths of many birds and the near-extinction of the species.

23

Gone Forever

Clues about the ancient creatures than once inhabited Earth are found only in remains, called fossils, buried in the ground. This might be teeth, bones, entire skeletons, or just the impression of a body in soil or silt. These animals died out mostly through natural evolution over millions of years. In recent centuries, however, some animals have been wiped out through human action.

Dead as a Dodo

Dodoes were giant, flightless pigeons that lived on the island of Mauritius in the Indian Ocean. They had no predators until Europeans arrived on the island in the fifteenth century, introducing pigs, dogs, rats, and cats that found the birds and their eggs easy prey. The dodo also provided easy food for passing sailors. By the seventeenth century, the dodo was extinct.

Beak

Dodoes had tiny wings and a large head with a hooked beak and a bald face. They lived on plants, seeds, and fruit.

Wing

Foot

24

It may be difficult to believe, but Andrewsarchus is closely related to today's hippopotamuses and whales!

Frightening Predator

In 1923, an ancient skull more than 3 ft (1 m) in length and with huge teeth was discovered in Mongolia. It belonged to an extinct animal that lived 35 million years ago, probably the largest meat-eating mammal ever. This gigantic creature, named Andrewsarchus, lived much like today's hyenas, scavenging for food, chasing away predators, and stealing their kill.

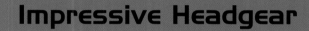

At one time, huge flocks of up to 2 billion passenger pigeons moved across the forests of North America, searching for acorns and nuts to eat. Settlers in the nineteenth century shot the birds for food and for sport. By 1900, the last bird was dead. Today, common pigeons (above) still make extraordinarily long-distance flights.

Impressive Headgear

Two million years ago, the giant deer, or Irish elk, roamed vast woodlands stretching from China to Ireland. The stags had huge antlers up to 13 ft (4 m) across. Fossilized antlers reveal marks where the stags locked them together in combat—just as they do today.

25

Legendary Creatures

There are legends of fantastic and fabulous creatures all over the world. Some were similar to actual living animals and resulted from attempts by early explorers to explain the wonders they had seen. Others remain mysteries that have yet to be solved.

Wing

If Looks Could Kill

The basilisk, from a Greek word meaning "little king," is a legendary creature with a dragon's wings and tail and a cockerel's head. Known as the king of serpents, the basilisk could drive away other serpents just by hissing, and both its breath and stare could be fatal.

Deadly breath

Tail

Only three things could kill a basilisk: a weasel, which was immune to the basilisk's deadly powers, a cock crowing, or its own reflection in a mirror.

26

Some mountaineers climbing in the Himalayas have claimed face-to-face encounters with a Yeti. Footprints, said to be those of the enormous creature, have often been photographed.

Beast on the Loose

Over the centuries, a number of part-ape, part-human creatures, such as the Bigfoot of North America, have been spotted, although none have ever been captured. The most famous of these is the Himalayan Yeti, or Abominable Snowman, said to live in the mountains of Nepal. Tests on hairs believed to have come from a Yeti suggest that the creature may be a kind of bear, related to the polar bear or brown bear.

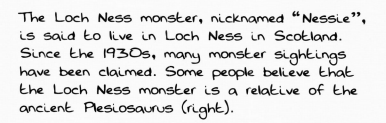

The Loch Ness monster, nicknamed "Nessie", is said to live in Loch Ness in Scotland. Since the 1930s, many monster sightings have been claimed. Some people believe that the Loch Ness monster is a relative of the ancient Plesiosaurus (right).

Mythical Guardian

The legendary griffin had a lion's body and an eagle's head and wings. The strange birds built their nests from gold, which they had to guard from raiders, such as a race of one-eyed giants called Arimaspians.

27

Incredible Creature Facts

Quite a Mouthful

The jaws of the Triceratops dinosaur had between 400 and 800 teeth. A human has no more than 32 teeth.

Long Lost Family

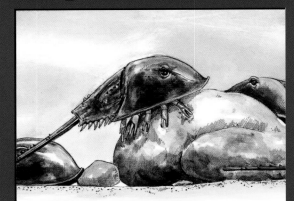

Horseshoe crabs are not actually related to crabs. Their closest relatives are sea scorpions that lived 300 million years ago.

Clam Trap

If a diver accidently stepped between the open shells of a giant clam, the creature's powerful muscles would contract quickly, snapping the shells closed around the diver's foot.

Deep-sea Diver

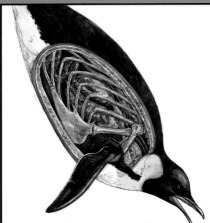

When they are in the ocean, emperor penguins can dive up to 1,850 ft (565 m), deeper than any other bird. The birds can stay underwater for more than 20 minutes.

Greedy Fish

The angler fish can extend its jaw and stretch its stomach so far that it can swallow other fish twice its size.

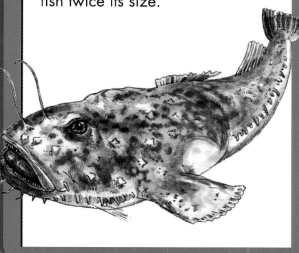

Taking it Easy

A sloth sleeps for up to 20 hours a day, curled up in a tree. It comes down from the tree only once a week. It does so for two reasons—to urinate and defecate!

Bat Crazy

Bats make up one fourth of all mammals. There are an incredible 1,100 species of bats on Earth.

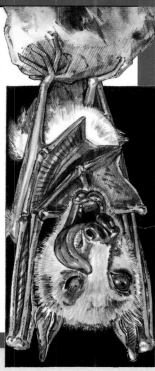

Super Ape

Orangutans can live for up to 45 years in the wild. The oldest recorded orangutan was a male named "Guas," who lived at Philadelphia Zoo. He reached the amazing age of 58.

29

Glossary

Cell a small unit of protoplasm surrounded by a thick skin, or membrane. All living things are made up of cells.

Cytoplasm the protoplasm of a cell, excluding the nucleus.

Evolved changed over a long period of time in order to survive.

Exoskeleton a rigid outer covering that protects the body of some animals. Insects and spiders are some of the animals that have an exoskeleton.

Extinction a process that leads to the loss of all animals in a species forever.

Fin the flattened limb of an animal that lives in water. Fins help propel animals through the water.

Fossil the remains of an ancient animal or plant.

Gills the organs through which water-living animals breathe.

30

Habitat the place in which an animal or plant lives.

Herbivore a plant-eating animal.

Larvae the young stage of an animal, such as an ant.

Mammal a warm-blooded animal that feeds its young with milk from its body. Mammals are usually covered in hair.

Membrane a protective layer that covers a living thing.

Nucleus the part of a cell that contains all the instructions it needs in order to function.

Predator an animal that hunts other animals.

Prey an animal that is hunted by other animals.

Index